ANDREW WYETH

23rd MAY – 22nd JUNE 1974

THE LEFEVRE GALLERY

ANDREW WYETH

FOREWORD

Ever since the late connoisseur-collector, Stephen C. Clark, stopped in at the Macbeth Gallery on Fifty-seventh Street in New York one day in 1948, saw CHRISTINA'S WORLD and bought it for the Museum of Modern Art, Andrew Wyeth's reputation has advanced with increasing speed so that today he is the most famous living American painter and surely the most loved. Various reasons have been advanced to account for Wyeth's popularity, none of them entirely satisfactory.

It goes without saying that Andrew Wyeth is the leading exponent of the realist tradition in American painting today and realism has rarely had to beg for devotees even in an age like ours dominated by abstraction. But it is not Wyeth's realism per se which accounts for his popularity, dazzled though we are by his skill and the depth of his observation. It is Andrew Wyeth's poetry and the values it celebrates that satisfy the yearnings of our age as the work of no other living American artist does. What we yearn for are those values that refute our materialism, oppose the encroachment of technological expansion and reject the madness of modern urban life. The art of Andrew Wyeth abounds in emblems which support these values, values that stir the heart of a tortured and disillusioned age.

Solitude, simple pleasures, rural folk, the unexpected beauty of the commonplace, nature serene and inviolate, the quietude of the country – this is the repertory of Andrew Wyeth which evokes an anti-materialist image of America and offers panacea to our spiritual blight.

The values reflected in Wyeth's art were his birthright. The youngest of five children, Andrew, was born July 12, 1917 at Chadd's Ford, Pennsylvania. Owing to his frail health he was taught at home by tutors and his parents. Most importantly, he came into daily contact with his father and his father's studio. N. C. Wyeth, one of the most distinguished illustrators of his time, was the formative influence in Andrew's boyhood. A hearty, exuberant, imaginative man, he believed in living life to the hilt and so he taught his children to be keen observers, to become intimate with nature to see the wonder in the humble and the commonplace. The elder Wyeth deliberately brought up his children to lead creative lives. He taught them to respect the life and thought of Henry David Thoreau. Hardly less emphasis was placed on those other American men-of-letters, Walt Whitman and Robert Frost. Among the artists Andrew most admired were Thomas Eakins for the honesty of his vision and Winslow Homer for the masculine strength of his watercolour washes and for his ability to perceive nature and extract its essence.

Wyeth's earliest paintings were in the watercolour medium. In them he sought for a fluent, liquid style expressed with spontaneity. He was searching for freshness, vigour; he wanted to display the 'handwriting' of the artist with his brush. But he found that the medium tempted him to virtuoso display at the expense of feeling. Moreover, detail became an increasingly important element in Wyeth's art and texture surpassed colour in its meaning to him. In consequence Wyeth's mature work has largely been expressed in the mediums of egg tempera and dry brush watercolour both of them more exacting but also more controllable and expressive of Wyeth's inspiration.

Altogether remarkable is the fact that all his life Wyeth has practised his art and drawn his inspiration from two small segments of his native land on the Atlantic seaboard, a few square miles in Pennsylvania and in Maine. He has never left America and has travelled very little in the United States. This is significant for it demonstrates the independence of the artist as well as his self-knowledge. 'It is not the country', he says, 'but what you carry to it that makes an artist'. The fibre and spirit of these two regions of America, his winter and summer homes, have insinuated themselves into his very blood stream. This union of artist and environment has yielded the works of art in this exhibition.

Andrew Wyeth has been a consistently creative artist for over thirty years. From the promise of his exuberant youthful paintings to the full maturity of the work of his present years, vibrant but sober and reflective, he has developed an art of increasing depth. Self-critical to a high degree, he has avoided the temptation of virtuoso display and has permitted his art to serve one thing only: his emotion about life. We respect him for this achievement, for his independence, for his truth to himself. His countless admirers in America (and elsewhere in the world: his retrospective exhibition opened at The National Museum of Modern Art in Tokyo last month) respond to the brilliance of his technique, the originality of his vision in theme and composition; they like his repertory of the humble and the common-place, his studies of human character, his whole-hearted love of nature, the 'nothingness' of his landscapes, his painstaking detail, his feeling for light, for texture, for white, for grey, for brown. But what else? All these characteristics of Wyeth's art are tangible, or at least describable. There remains however a transcendent element in his painting that is subtle, elusive, beyond description. Almost all of Wyeth's works are haunted by an unseen presence which is the more palpable for the silence that envelops them. He imbues the fleeting moment for which he strives with a tense, brooding quality that transforms the innocent, the ostensible reality which he appears to depict. Wyeth is a deeply subjective man. To an extraordinary degree he identifies himself with whatever theme he undertakes to develop. His personal associations, often stored in his memory for many years, surge up to suffuse these chosen themes with deep emotion. What then is this intangible that we sense in the thick of reality? It is the subjective feeling of one particular human being – the deep sincere but private intimations of Andrew Wyeth. Herein lies his ultimate fascination, his magic.

PERRY T. RATHBONE*

* Perry T. Rathbone is Director Emeritus of The Museum of Fine Arts, Boston and is now Director of Christie's USA, in New York

INDEX

**WATERCOLOUR STUDIES
AND PENCIL DRAWINGS**

14 **Turkey Pond, 1944**
$6\frac{3}{4} \times 7\frac{3}{4}$ inches

15 **Picking Apples, 1945**
$20\frac{3}{4} \times 28\frac{3}{4}$ inches

16 **A Crow Flew by, 1950**
13×19 inches

17 **The Boot, 1951**
7×8 inches

18 **Milk Pails, 1953**
$5\frac{1}{4} \times 5\frac{3}{4}$ inches

19 **Snow Flurries, 1953**
13×19 inches

20 **Basket of Apples, 1957**
14×22 inches

21 **Adam, 1963**
$16\frac{1}{2} \times 23\frac{1}{2}$ inches

22 **Buzzard's Glory, 1968**
$13\frac{1}{4} \times 16\frac{1}{2}$ inches

TEMPERA

1 IDES OF MARCH

Tempera
$24\frac{1}{2} \times 41\frac{1}{2}$ inches
Signed upper right
Painted in 1974

No. 1.

7

DRY BRUSH AND WATERCOLOURS

2 ALEXANDER CHANDLER

Dry brush
21½ × 15 inches
Signed lower right
Painted in 1955

Literature   Eliot Clark, Studio Magazine, 'Andrew Wyeth, America's Most
Popular Painter', December, 1960, page 209
Jay Jacobs, Art in America, 'Andrew Wyeth, An Unsentimental
Reappraisal', January–February, 1967, page 30
Richard Meryman, Gambit, Inc. 'Andrew Wyeth', 1969, page 32
Richard Meryman, 'Andrew Wyeth', Boston 1968, reproduced in
colour, plate 28

Exhibited   New York, K. Knoedler & Co., 'Andrew Wyeth, Recent Paintings',
October 28th–November 22nd, 1958, No. 39
Buffalo, New York, Albright-Knox Art Gallery, 'Andrew Wyeth –
Temperas, Watercolours and Drawings', November 2nd–December
9th, 1962, No. 112
Philadelphia, Pennsylvania Academy of the Fine Arts, 'Andrew
Wyeth', October 8th–November 27th, 1966, page 50
Baltimore Maryland, Baltimore Museum of Art, December 13th 1966–
January 22nd, 1967, page 51, No. 75
New York, Whitney Museum of American Art, February 14th–
April 2nd, 1967, page 51, No. 75
Chicago, Illinois, The Art Institute of Chicago, April 21st–June 4th,
1967, page 51, No. 75
Bamberger's 4th Annual Holiday Art Exhibition, 1969, No. 25
Boston, Massachusetts, Boston Museum of Fine Arts, 1970, page 81,
No. 30
San Francisco, The M. H. de Young Memorial Museum of Fine
Arts, 'The Art of Andrew Wyeth', June 16th–September 3rd, 1973,
illustrated in colour page 147

Collection   Mr. & Mrs. Robert Montgomery, New York

No. 13

WATERCOLOUR STUDIES AND PENCIL DRAWINGS

14 TURKEY POND
   (Prestudy for tempera 'Turkey Pond')
   (40¼ × 32¼ inches)

Dry brush
6¾ × 7¾ inches
Signed lower right
Painted in 1944

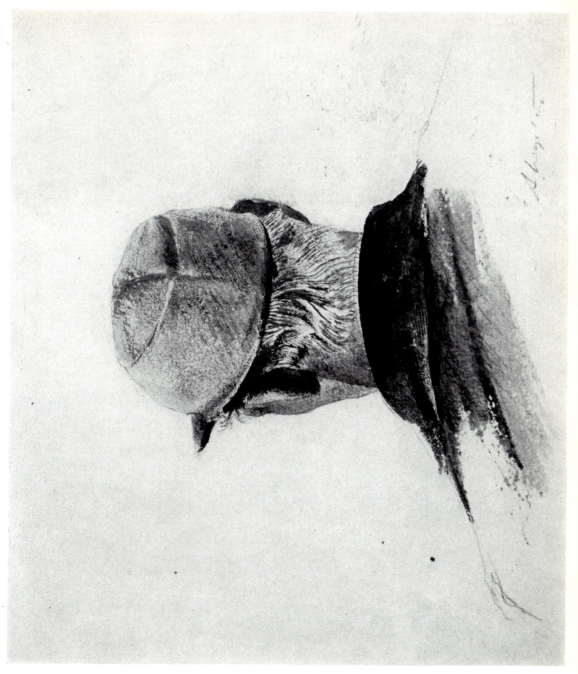

No. 14

33

15 PICKING APPLES

Watercolour
$20\frac{3}{4} \times 28\frac{3}{4}$ inches
Signed lower right
Painted in 1945

16 A CROW FLEW BY
(Prestudy for tempera 'A Crow Flew by', 1949–50)
($17\frac{1}{2} \times 27$ inches)

Pencil drawing
13×19 inches
Signed lower centre
Painted in 1950

No. 15

No. 16

17 THE BOOT

(Prestudy for tempera 'The Trodden Weed 1951)

(20 × 18⅜ inches)

Pencil drawing
7 × 8 inches
Signed lower right
Painted in 1951

18 MILK PAILS

(Prestudy for tempera 'Monday Morning' c. 1955)

(12 × 16⅜ inches)

Pencil drawing
5¼ × 5¾ inches
Unsigned
Painted in 1953

No. 17

No. 18

19 SNOW FLURRIES
(Prestudy for tempera 'Snow Flurries' 1953)
($37\frac{1}{4} \times 48$ inches)

Pencil Drawing
13×19 inches
Signed lower right
Painted in 1953

20 BASKET OF APPLES

Pencil Drawing
14×22 inches
Signed lower right
Painted in 1957

No. 19

No. 20

39

21   **ADAM**
  (Prestudy for tempera 'Adam' 1963)
  (24½ × 48 inches)

                                   Watercolour
                                   16½ × 23½ inches
                                   Unsigned
                                   Painted in 1963

22   **BUZZARD'S GLORY**
  (Prestudy for tempera 'Buzzard's Glory' 1968)
  (18 × 23⅜ inches)

                                   Pencil drawing
                                   13¼ × 16½ inches
                                   Unsigned
                                   Painted in 1968

No. 21

No. 22

No. 2

9

3 INDEPENDENCE DAY

Watercolour
14 × 20 inches
Signed lower left
Painted in 1961

No. 3.

4 THE FALLS ON GOOSE RIVER
   (Prestudy for tempera 'The Intruder' 1971)
   ($30\frac{1}{2} \times 50$ inches)

Dry brush
$21\frac{3}{4} \times 39\frac{1}{8}$ inches
Signed lower left
Painted in 1970–71

No. 4.

5 KNOX'S ARTILLERY

Watercolour
$21\frac{3}{8} \times 29$ inches
Signed lower left
Painted in 1972

6 PINES IN THE SNOW

Watercolour
$21\frac{1}{8} \times 29\frac{1}{8}$ inches
Signed lower right
Painted in 1972

7   THE VESTRY
(Prestudy for tempera 'Off at Sea' 1972)
(37 × 37 inches)

Dry brush
25⅛ × 36¾ inches
Signed lower right
Painted in 1972

No. 7

8   CIRCUS DAY

Watercolour
30 × 22 inches
Signed upper right
Painted in 1973

9 JACK AND WILLARD

Watercolour
$21\frac{3}{8} \times 29\frac{1}{4}$ inches
Signed lower right
Painted in 1973

23

10 LATE HARVEST

Watercolour
$21\frac{3}{4} \times 30$ inches
Signed lower right
Painted in 1973

No. 10

11 SIX POUNDER

Watercolour
21 × 29 inches
Signed lower right
Painted in 1973

No. 11

12 SLEET STORM

Watercolour
$18\frac{1}{4} \times 29\frac{3}{4}$ inches
Signed lower left
Painted in 1973

No. 12

13 TURNER'S MILL

Watercolour
$29\frac{1}{2} \times 21\frac{1}{2}$ inches
Unsigned
Painted in 1973

26.119